Neural Network Programming with Python

Create your own neural network!

Table of Contents

Introduction

The need for neural networks in society is on the rise. This is the case in most production environments. That is why there is a need for you to know how to implement these. The Python programming language provides you with a number of libraries which you can use for the purpose of implementing neural networks. These libraries are easy for you to use, and you just use a few simple steps so as to implement your own neural network. These are discussed in this book. Enjoy reading!

Chapter 1- A Brief Overview of Neural Networks

Neural networks are represented in the form of a mathematical model, and they are mostly applied in machine learning. They are made up of neurons which are connected to each other, and these usually send each other signal. The neuron has to receive the signals until they exceed its threshold, and this is when it fires, meaning that it forwards the signal to the next connected neuron in the network. The connections between the neurons can be done in the way we want, even to the same neuron, but the problem comes in when we need to train the network, and this explains why restrictions have to be imposed on the creation of neural networks.

In the case of a multi-layer perceptron, the neurons have been arranged into layers, and each neuron is allowed to pass signals only to the next neuron in the layer. The first layer in this is the input layer, while the last one is the output layer, and this will have the predicted values.

Chapter 2- Backpropagation Algorithm

The backpropagation algorithm is used for the implementation of neural networks in Python. This algorithm has two phases:

1. Forward pass- whereby the training data is run through the network so as to obtain the output.

2. Backward pass- whereby we start from the output, and then calculate the error for each neuron, and these are used for adjusting the weight of the network.

We want to demonstrate how a neural network is implemented in Python. We should begin by defining the activation functions and their derivatives, whereby we use Numpy. This is shown below:

```
import numpy as np

def tanh(x):
  return np.tanh(x)

def tanh_deriv(x):
  return 1.0 - np.tanh(x)**2

def logistic(x):
  return 1/(1 + np.exp(-x))

def logistic_derivative(y):
  return logistic(y)*(1-logistic(y))
```

The number of neurons in each of our layers should be defined in the constructor for the class. Their weights should also be initialized randomly and set the activation function which is to be used. The weights should range between -0.25 and 0.25. Each of the layers, with the exception of the last one, should have a bias unit corresponding to the threshold value for our activation. This is shown below:

```python
class NeuralNetwork:
    def __init__(self, layers, activation='tanh'):
        """

        :param layers: A list having the number of units
        in each of the layers.

        Should have at least two values
        :param activation: The activation function we
        need to use. Can be
        "logistic" or "tanh"
        """
        if activation == 'logistic':
            self.activation = logistic
            self.activation_deriv = logistic_derivative
        elif activation == 'tanh':
            self.activation = tanh
            self.activation_deriv = tanh_deriv

        self.weights = []
        for i in range(1, len(layers) - 1):

            self.weights.append((2*np.random.random((layers[i
            - 1] + 1, layers[i

                    + 1))-1)*0.25)

            self.weights.append((2*np.random.random((layers[i
            ] + 1, layers[i +

                    1]))-1)*0.25)
```

After setting that, we get into training the neural network. Once you are given a set of input vectors as X and the output as Y, you should adjust the weight as expected. We will use the stochastic gradient descent algorithm which will randomly choose a sample from our training data and then perform a back propagation for the sample, and this will have to be repeated for a number of times. The learning rate of the algorithm should also be set, and this will determine the amount of change that occurs in our weights each time. This should be proportional to the errors as shown below:

```
def fit(self, X, y, learning_rate=0.2, epochs=10000):
    X = np.atleast_2d(X)
    temp = np.ones([X.shape[0], X.shape[1]+1])
    temp[:, 0:-1] = X  # add the bias unit to input layer
    X = temp
    y = np.array(y)

    for k in range(epochs):
        i = np.random.randint(X.shape[0])
        a = [X[i]]

        for l in range(len(self.weights)):
            a.append(self.activation(np.dot(a[l],
self.weights[l])))
        error = y[i] - a[-1]
        deltas = [error * self.activation_deriv(a[-1])]

        for l in range(len(a) - 2, 0, -1): # we should
begin at the second to our last layer

            deltas.append(deltas[-
1].dot(self.weights[l].T)*self.activation_deriv(a[l]))

        deltas.reverse()
        for i in range(len(self.weights)):
            layer = np.atleast_2d(a[i])
            delta = np.atleast_2d(deltas[i])
```

```
    self.weights[i] += learning_rate *
layer.T.dot(delta)
```

After training, we get to the part for prediction. This works in a similar manner as the forward pass in the backpropagation algorithm, with the exception being that we will have to keep all the values for the activations for each of our neurons, so we will have to keep only the last one. This is shown below:

```
def predict(self, x):
    x = np.array(x)
    temp = np.ones(x.shape[0]+1)
    temp[0:-1] = x
    a = temp
    for l in range(0, len(self.weights)):
        a = self.activation(np.dot(a, self.weights[l]))
    return a
```

That will be over. We have 50 lines of code for our neural network, plus 10 for the activation functions. We can now test it.

We will begin by using the XOR function to test. The function is not linearly separable once it has been represented in a plane, and there exists no line which can separate the points with the label 1 from our points with the label 0, meaning that we should have   at least one hidden layer. That is why we should use 2 units as shown below:

```
n = NeuralNetwork([2,2,1], 'tanh')
X = np.array([[0, 0], [0, 1], [1, 0], [1, 1]])
y = np.array([0, 1, 1, 0])
n.fit(X, y)
for i in [[0, 0], [0, 1], [1, 0], [1,1]]:
    print(i,n.predict(i))
```

We should then get the following as the output:

([0, 0], array([4.01282568e-05]))

([0, 1], array([0.98765949]))
([1, 0], array([0.98771753]))
([1, 1], array([0.00490502]))

That is good. If we had used a step function for the activations in our output layers, we would be able to extract the results.

We now need to look at something which is a bit complicated. The scikit-learn was part of the digits dataset which we got. This has the digits for 1797 8x8 pixel images in the labels. We need to check the kind of accuracy that we can get from this. The labels should be transformed from the values that we have to the vectors of 10 elements. This is shown below:

```
import numpy as np
from sklearn.cross_validation import
train_test_split
from NeuralNetwork import NeuralNetwork
from sklearn.metrics import confusion_matrix,
classification_report

from sklearn.datasets import load_digits
from sklearn.preprocessing import LabelBinarizer

digits = load_digits()
X = digits.data
y = digits.target
X -= X.min() # normalizing the values to have them in
the range 0-1
X /= X.max()

n = NeuralNetwork([64,100,10],'tanh')
X_train, X_test, y_train, y_test = train_test_split(X,
y)
labels_train =
LabelBinarizer().fit_transform(y_train)
labels_test = LabelBinarizer().fit_transform(y_test)

nn.fit(X_train,labels_train,epochs=30000)
```

```
predictions = []
for i in range(X_test.shape[0]):
    o = n.predict(X_test[i] )
    predictions.append(np.argmax(o))
print confusion_matrix(y_test,predictions)
print classification_report(y_test,predictions)
```

In the output, we will get a confusion matrix and a very nice report as shown below:

```
[[50  0  0  0  0  0  0  0  0  0]
 [ 0 39  1  0  0  0  0  1  2  6]
 [ 0  0 52  0  0  0  0  0  0  0]
 [ 0  0  2 34  0  1  0  0  5  0]
 [ 0  1  0  0 35  0  1  1  0  0]
 [ 0  0  0  0  0 50  1  0  0  1]
 [ 0  0  0  0  0  0 37  0  4  0]
 [ 0  0  0  0  0  0  0 47  0  1]
 [ 0  0  0  0  0  1  1  0 38  1]
 [ 0  0  1  0  0  1  0  1  1 33]]
```
precision   recall f1-score   support

0 1.00 1.00 1.00 50
1 0.97 0.80 0.88 49
2 0.93 1.00 0.96 52
3 1.00 0.81 0.89 42
4 1.00 0.92 0.96 38
5 0.94 0.96 0.95 52
6 0.93 0.90 0.91 41
7 0.94 0.98 0.96 48
8 0.76 0.93 0.84 41
9 0.79 0.89 0.84 37

avg / total 0.93 0.92 0.92 450

We have got a 93% accuracy, which is very good for a 50 line of code model with no optimizations implemented. There are a number of things which we could have done so as to make an improvement to our models, such as the addition of momentum, regularization, and other things.

A Toy Example

We need to create a toy example which one can play with. This can be implemented by use of the backpropagation algorithm in Python. Consider the code given below:

```
X = np.array([ [0,0,1],[0,1,1],[1,0,1],[1,1,1] ])
y = np.array([[0,1,1,0]]).T
syn0 = 2*np.random.random((3,4)) - 1
syn1 = 2*np.random.random((4,1)) - 1
for j in xrange(60000):
    l1 = 1/(1+np.exp(-(np.dot(X,syn0))))
    l2 = 1/(1+np.exp(-(np.dot(l1,syn1))))
    l2_delta = (y - l2)*(l2*(1-l2))
    l1_delta = l2_delta.dot(syn1.T) * (l1 * (1-l1))
    syn1 += l1.T.dot(l2_delta)
    syn0 += X.T.dot(l1_delta)
```

The code may seem to be tough to you. We need to break it into parts. In this case, we need to use the backpropagation algorithm so as to take an input and predict the output. This is mostly done by measuring of the statistics found between the input and the output. This can help you to easily know the correlation between the input and the output values. Let us demonstrate how the algorithm for predicting this works:

```
import numpy as np

# sigmoid function
def nonlin(x,deriv=False):
    if(deriv==True):
        return x*(1-x)
    return 1/(1+np.exp(-x))
```

```
# the input dataset
X = np.array([ [0,0,1],
        [0,1,1],
        [1,0,1],
        [1,1,1] ])

# the output dataset
y = np.array([[0,0,1,1]]).T

# the seed random numbers for making calculation
# the deterministic (a good practice)
np.random.seed(1)

# initializing the weights randomly with a mean of 0
syn0 = 2*np.random.random((3,1)) - 1

for iter in xrange(10000):

    # the forward pass
    l0 = X
    l1 = nonlin(np.dot(l0,syn0))

    # how much have we missed?
    l1_error = y - l1

    # multiplying how much we have missed by the
    # slope of our sigmoid at our values in l1
    l1_delta = l1_error * nonlin(l1,True)

    # updating the weights
    syn0 += np.dot(l0.T,l1_delta)

print "The output After Training:"
print l1
```

The code should give you the following as the output:

```
[[ 0.00966449]
 [ 0.00786506]
```

[0.99358898]
[0.99211957]]

A 3 Layer Neural Network

Consider the code given below:

```python
import numpy as np

def nonlin(x,deriv=False):
        if(deriv==True):
            return x*(1-x)

        return 1/(1+np.exp(-x))

X = np.array([[0,0,1],
        [0,1,1],
        [1,0,1],
        [1,1,1]])

y = np.array([[0],
                    [1],
                    [1],
                    [0]])

np.random.seed(1)

# randomly initializing the weights with a mean of 0
syn0 = 2*np.random.random((3,4)) - 1
syn1 = 2*np.random.random((4,1)) - 1

for j in xrange(60000):

        # A Feed forward through the layers 0, 1, and
2
    l0 = X
    l1 = nonlin(np.dot(l0,syn0))
    l2 = nonlin(np.dot(l1,syn1))

    # how much have we missed the target value?
    l2_error = y - l2
```

```
if (j% 10000) == 0:
    print "Error:" + str(np.mean(np.abs(l2_error)))

# To what direction is our target value?
# were we sure? if so, do not change very much.
l2_delta = l2_error*nonlin(l2,deriv=True)

# how much did each of the l1 value contribute to l2
error (according to our weights)?

l1_error = l2_delta.dot(syn1.T)

# to what direction is target l1?
# were we sure? if so, do not change very much.
l1_delta = l1_error * nonlin(l1,deriv=True)

syn1 += l1.T.dot(l2_delta)
syn0 += l0.T.dot(l1_delta)
```

The code should give you the following:

```
Error:0.496410031903
Error:0.00858452565325
Error:0.00578945986251
Error:0.00462917677677
Error:0.00395876528027
Error:0.00351012256786
```

Gradient Descent

Consider the code given below:

```
import numpy as np
X = np.array([ [0,0,1],[0,1,1],[1,0,1],[1,1,1] ])
y = np.array([[0,1,1,0]]).T
alpha,hidden_dim = (0.5,4)
synapse_0 = 2*np.random.random((3,hidden_dim))
- 1
```

```python
synapse_1 = 2*np.random.random((hidden_dim,1)) -
1
for j in xrange(60000):
    layer_1 = 1/(1+np.exp(-(np.dot(X,synapse_0))))
    layer_2 = 1/(1+np.exp(-
(np.dot(layer_1,synapse_1))))
    layer_2_delta = (layer_2 - y)*(layer_2*(1-layer_2))
    layer_1_delta = layer_2_delta.dot(synapse_1.T) *
(layer_1 * (1-layer_1))

    synapse_1 -= (alpha * layer_1.T.dot(layer_2_delta))
    synapse_0 -= (alpha * X.T.dot(layer_1_delta))
```

You should remember that backpropagation does not perform optimization. It just moves the information regarding the error from the end of your network to the weights contained inside the network so that the weights can be optimized by a different algorithm so as to fit the data.

2 Layer Neural Network

Consider the code given below:

```
import numpy as np

# computing the sigmoid nonlinearity
def sigmoid(x):
    output = 1/(1+np.exp(-x))
    return output

# converting the output of the sigmoid function to get
its derivative
def sigmoid_output_to_derivative(output):
    return output*(1-output)

# the input dataset
X = np.array([ [0,1],
        [0,1],
        [1,0],
        [1,0] ])

# the output dataset
y = np.array([[0,0,1,1]]).T

# the seed random numbers for making the
calculation
# a deterministic ( a very good practice)
np.random.seed(1)

# initializing the weights randomly with a mean of 0
synapse_0 = 2*np.random.random((2,1)) - 1

for iter in xrange(10000):

    # the forward pass
    layer_0 = X
    layer_1 = sigmoid(np.dot(layer_0,synapse_0))
```

```python
    # how much have we missed?
    layer_1_error = layer_1 - y

    # multiplying how much we have missed by the
    # slope of our sigmoid at values in l1
    layer_1_delta = layer_1_error *
sigmoid_output_to_derivative(layer_1)
    synapse_0_derivative =
np.dot(layer_0.T,layer_1_delta)

    # updating the weights
    synapse_0 -= synapse_0_derivative

print "Output After the Training:"
print layer_1
```

That is a 2 layered network that can be implemented in Python.

Consider the next code given below:

```python
import numpy as np

alphas = [0.001,0.01,0.1,1,10,100,1000]

# computing the sigmoid nonlinearity
def sigmoid(x):
    output = 1/(1+np.exp(-x))
    return output

# converting the output of our sigmoid function to get
its derivative
def sigmoid_output_to_derivative(output):
    return output*(1-output)

X = np.array([[0,0,1],
        [0,1,1],
        [1,0,1],
```

```
           [1,1,1]])

y = np.array([[0],
                          [1],
                          [1],
                          [0]])

for alpha in alphas:
    print "\nTraining With Alpha:" + str(alpha)
    np.random.seed(1)

    # randomly initializing our weights with a mean of
0
    synapse_0 = 2*np.random.random((3,4)) - 1
    synapse_1 = 2*np.random.random((4,1)) - 1

    for j in xrange(60000):

        # Feed forward through the layers 0, 1, and 2
        layer_0 = X
        layer_1 = sigmoid(np.dot(layer_0,synapse_0))
        layer_2 = sigmoid(np.dot(layer_1,synapse_1))

        # how much have we miss in the target value?
        layer_2_error = layer_2 - y

        if (j% 10000) == 0:
            print "Error after "+str(j)+" iterations:" +
str(np.mean(np.abs(layer_2_error)))

        # in which direction is our target value?
        # were we sure? if so, do not change very much.
        layer_2_delta =
layer_2_error*sigmoid_output_to_derivative(layer_
2)

        # how much did each of the l1 value contribute to
l2 error (according to our weights)?
```

```
    layer_1_error = layer_2_delta.dot(synapse_1.T)

    # in which direction is our target l1?
    # were we sure? if so, do not change very much.
    layer_1_delta = layer_1_error *
sigmoid_output_to_derivative(layer_1)

    synapse_1 -= alpha *
(layer_1.T.dot(layer_2_delta))

    synapse_0 -= alpha *
(layer_0.T.dot(layer_1_delta))
```

The above code is for an improved gradient descent. Note that we have used different values for the alpha variable. If we use very small sizes for the alpha variable, the network will hardly converge.

Consider the next code given below:

```
import numpy as np

alphas = [0.001,0.01,0.1,1,10,100,1000]

# computing the sigmoid nonlinearity
def sigmoid(x):
    output = 1/(1+np.exp(-x))
    return output

# converting the output of the sigmoid function to get
its derivative

def sigmoid_output_to_derivative(output):
    return output*(1-output)

X = np.array([[0,0,1],
    [0,1,1],
    [1,0,1],
    [1,1,1]])
```

```python
y = np.array([[0],
              [1],
              [1],
              [0]])

for alpha in alphas:
    print "\nTraining With the Alpha:" + str(alpha)
    np.random.seed(1)

    # randomly initializing our weights with a mean of
0
    synapse_0 = 2*np.random.random((3,4)) - 1
    synapse_1 = 2*np.random.random((4,1)) - 1

    prev_synapse_0_weight_update =
np.zeros_like(synapse_0)
    prev_synapse_1_weight_update =
np.zeros_like(synapse_1)

    synapse_0_direction_count =
np.zeros_like(synapse_0)
    synapse_1_direction_count =
np.zeros_like(synapse_1)

    for j in xrange(60000):

        # Feed forward through the layers 0, 1, and 2
        layer_0 = X
        layer_1 = sigmoid(np.dot(layer_0,synapse_0))
        layer_2 = sigmoid(np.dot(layer_1,synapse_1))

        # how much have we missed the target value?
        layer_2_error = y - layer_2

        if (j% 10000) == 0:
            print "Error:" +
str(np.mean(np.abs(layer_2_error)))
```

```python
        # in which direction is our target value?
        # were we sure? if so, do not change very much.
        layer_2_delta =
layer_2_error*sigmoid_output_to_derivative(layer_
2)

        # how much did each of the l1 values contribute to
l2 error (according to our weights)?

        layer_1_error = layer_2_delta.dot(synapse_1.T)

        # in which direction is our target l1?
        # were we sure? if so, do not change very much.
        layer_1_delta = layer_1_error *
sigmoid_output_to_derivative(layer_1)

        synapse_1_weight_update =
(layer_1.T.dot(layer_2_delta))
        synapse_0_weight_update =
(layer_0.T.dot(layer_1_delta))

        if(j > 0):
            synapse_0_direction_count +=
np.abs(((synapse_0_weight_update > 0)+0) -
((prev_synapse_0_weight_update > 0) + 0))

            synapse_1_direction_count +=
np.abs(((synapse_1_weight_update > 0)+0) -
((prev_synapse_1_weight_update > 0) + 0))

        synapse_1 += alpha * synapse_1_weight_update
        synapse_0 += alpha * synapse_0_weight_update

        prev_synapse_0_weight_update =
synapse_0_weight_update
        prev_synapse_1_weight_update =
synapse_1_weight_update
```

```
print "Synapse 0"
print synapse_0

print "Synapse 0 to Update Direction Changes"
print synapse_0_direction_count

print "Synapse 1"
print synapse_1

print "Synapse 1 to Update Direction Changes"
print synapse_1_direction_count
```

In our above example, we have counted the number of times that a derivative changes direction. In case our slope changes its direction, this is just an indication that it has passed over the local minimum and it is in need of going back. In case it fails to change direction, then this will be an indication that it has not gone far.

Parameterizing the Hidden Layer Size

If we are in a position to increase the size of our hidden layer, then this will be an indication that we will be in a position to increase the search space that we are able to converge to during each of the iterations. Consider the network given below:

```
import numpy as np

alphas = [0.001,0.01,0.1,1,10,100,1000]
hiddenSize = 32

# computing the sigmoid nonlinearity
def sigmoid(x):
    output = 1/(1+np.exp(-x))
    return output

# converting the output of the sigmoid function to get
its derivative
```

```
def sigmoid_output_to_derivative(output):
    return output*(1-output)

X = np.array([[0,0,1],
        [0,1,1],
        [1,0,1],
        [1,1,1]])

y = np.array([[0],
                [1],
                [1],
                [0]])

for alpha in alphas:
    print "\nTraining With the Alpha:" + str(alpha)
    np.random.seed(1)

    # randomly initializing the weights with a mean of 0
    synapse_0 = 2*np.random.random((3,hiddenSize))
- 1
    synapse_1 = 2*np.random.random((hiddenSize,1))
- 1

    for j in xrange(60000):

        # Feed forward through layers 0, 1, and 2
        layer_0 = X
        layer_1 = sigmoid(np.dot(layer_0,synapse_0))
        layer_2 = sigmoid(np.dot(layer_1,synapse_1))

        # how much have we missed the target value?
        layer_2_error = layer_2 - y

        if (j% 10000) == 0:
            print "Error after some"+str(j)+" iterations:" +
str(np.mean(np.abs(layer_2_error)))

        # in which direction is our target value?
```

```python
    # were we sure? if so, do not change very much.
    layer_2_delta =
layer_2_error*sigmoid_output_to_derivative(layer_
2)

    # how much did each of l1 value contribute to l2
error (according to our weights)?

    layer_1_error = layer_2_delta.dot(synapse_1.T)

    # in which direction is our target l1?
    # were we sure? if so, do not change very much.
    layer_1_delta = layer_1_error *
sigmoid_output_to_derivative(layer_1)

    synapse_1 -= alpha *
(layer_1.T.dot(layer_2_delta))
    synapse_0 -= alpha *
(layer_0.T.dot(layer_1_delta))
```

Neural Network Memory

Below is the code for this:

```python
import copy, numpy as np
np.random.seed(0)

# computing the sigmoid nonlinearity
def sigmoid(x):
    output = 1/(1+np.exp(-x))
    return output

# converting the output of the sigmoid function to get
its derivative
def sigmoid_output_to_derivative(output):
    return output*(1-output)
```

```python
# training generation of the dataset
int2binary = {}
binary_dim = 8

largest_number = pow(2,binary_dim)
binary = np.unpackbits(

np.array([range(largest_number)],dtype=np.uint8).
T,axis=1)
for i in range(largest_number):
    int2binary[i] = binary[i]

# the input variables
alpha = 0.1
input_dim = 2
hidden_dim = 16
output_dim = 1

# initializing the neural network weights
synapse_0 =
2*np.random.random((input_dim,hidden_dim)) - 1
synapse_1 =
2*np.random.random((hidden_dim,output_dim)) - 1
synapse_h =
2*np.random.random((hidden_dim,hidden_dim)) - 1

synapse_0_update = np.zeros_like(synapse_0)
synapse_1_update = np.zeros_like(synapse_1)
synapse_h_update = np.zeros_like(synapse_h)

# training logic
for j in range(10000):

    # generating a simple addition problem (a + b = c)
    a_int = np.random.randint(largest_number/2) #
int version
    a = int2binary[a_int] # binary encoding
```

```python
    b_int = np.random.randint(largest_number/2) #
int version
    b = int2binary[b_int] # binary encoding

    # the true answer
    c_int = a_int + b_int
    c = int2binary[c_int]

    # where to store the best guess (binary encoded)
    d = np.zeros_like(c)

    overallError = 0

    layer_2_deltas = list()
    layer_1_values = list()
    layer_1_values.append(np.zeros(hidden_dim))

    # move along positions in binary encoding
    for position in range(binary_dim):

        # generate the input and the output
        X = np.array([[a[binary_dim - position -
1],b[binary_dim - position - 1]]])

        y = np.array([[c[binary_dim - position - 1]]]).T

        # our hidden layer (input ~+ prev_hidden)
        layer_1 = sigmoid(np.dot(X,synapse_0) +
np.dot(layer_1_values[-1],synapse_h))

        # our output layer (binary representation, new)
        layer_2 = sigmoid(np.dot(layer_1,synapse_1))

        # have we missed?... if so, then by how much?
        layer_2_error = y - layer_2

layer_2_deltas.append((layer_2_error)*sigmoid_out
put_to_derivative(layer_2))
```

```python
        overallError += np.abs(layer_2_error[0])

        # decode the estimate so as to print it out
        d[binary_dim - position - 1] =
np.round(layer_2[0][0])

        # store the hidden layer so as to use it in our next
timestep
        layer_1_values.append(copy.deepcopy(layer_1))

    future_layer_1_delta = np.zeros(hidden_dim)

    for position in range(binary_dim):

        X = np.array([[a[position],b[position]]])
        layer_1 = layer_1_values[-position-1]
        prev_layer_1 = layer_1_values[-position-2]
        # error at the output layer
        layer_2_delta = layer_2_deltas[-position-1]
        # error at the hidden layer
        layer_1_delta =
(future_layer_1_delta.dot(synapse_h.T) +
layer_2_delta.dot(synapse_1.T)) *
sigmoid_output_to_derivative(layer_1)

        # let us update all the weights to try again
        synapse_1_update +=
np.atleast_2d(layer_1).T.dot(layer_2_delta)

        synapse_h_update +=
np.atleast_2d(prev_layer_1).T.dot(layer_1_delta)
        synapse_0_update += X.T.dot(layer_1_delta)

        future_layer_1_delta = layer_1_delta

    synapse_0 += synapse_0_update * alpha
    synapse_1 += synapse_1_update * alpha
    synapse_h += synapse_h_update * alpha
    synapse_0_update *= 0
```

```python
        synapse_1_update *= 0
        synapse_h_update *= 0
        # print out the progress
        if(j % 1000 == 0):
            print "Error:" + str(overallError)
            print "Pred:" + str(d)
            print "True:" + str(c)
            out = 0
            for index,x in enumerate(reversed(d)):
                out += x*pow(2,index)
            print str(a_int) + " + " + str(b_int) + " = " +
str(out)
            print "------------"
```

Chapter 3- Neural Networks with Numpy

Neural networks are just machine learning algorithms which are used for classification. They may seem to be intimidating to learn, which is not the case. Their name is from the neurons in human brain, as they have a similar functionality.

The activation function of a neuron determines whether it is "on" or "off." We need to use a sigmoid function which is very easy as a result of logistic regression. A derivative of a neural network is also needed when we are working with a neural net. This is shown in the code given below:

```
import numpy as np
def sigmoid(x):
    return 1 / (1 + np.exp(-x))
# derivative of a sigmoid
# sigmoid(y) * (1.0 - sigmoid(y))
# the way  this y should be used is already sigmoided
def dsigmoid(y):
    return y * (1.0 - y)
```

A sigmoid function in a neural network generates the endpoint of the inputs multiplied by their weights. An example of this is when we have two columns of the input data and one hidden node in the neural network. Each feature has to be multiplied by the corresponding value of the weight, added together, and then passed through the sigmoid. We should add more hidden units so that the example can be turned into a neural network. In addition to that, a path should be added from every input feature to the hidden units, and then multiplied by the corresponding weights. Each of the hidden units will take the sum of the sum of the inputs multiply by the weights and then pass through the sigmoid so as to get the activation for that unit.

We can then setup arrays which will hold the data for our network and then initialize the parameters. This is shown below:

```python
class MLP_NeuralNetwork(object):
    def __init__(self, input, hidden, output):
        """
        :param input: number of your input neurons
        :param hidden: number of the hidden neurons
        :param output: number of the output neurons
        """
        self.input = input + 1 # add 1 for the bias node
        self.hidden = hidden
        self.output = output
        # set up an array of 1s for the activations
        self.ai = [1.0] * self.input
        self.ah = [1.0] * self.hidden
        self.ao = [1.0] * self.output
        # create randomized weights
        self.wi = np.random.randn(self.input,
self.hidden)
        self.wo = np.random.randn(self.hidden,
self.output)
        # creating arrays of 0 for the changes
        self.ci = np.zeros((self.input, self.hidden))
        self.co = np.zeros((self.hidden, self.output))
```

The calculations will be done through matrices because of their ease of use. Our class is expected to take three inputs, that is, size of input layer, size of hidden layer, and number of output layers. An array of 1s should be setup as a placeholder for unit activations, and then an array of 0s for the changes in the layer. Remember that all our weights had been initialized to random numbers. This is of importance, as it will allow us to tune the weight of our network. If you use the same weight, then the hidden units will be the same, and we will be screwed.

At this point, we can make some predictions. We should forward all the data through the network with random weights and then make some predictions. Later, once we have made each prediction, we can calculate how wrong they are and determine the direction that we need to make the changes so as to make better predictions. We should come up with a feed forward function which we can call for a number of times. Consider the code given below:

```
def feedForwardFunc(self, inputs):
  if len(inputs) != self.input-1:
    raise ValueError('You have wrong number of inputs!')
  # input activations
  for i in range(self.input -1): # -1 is for avoiding the bias
    self.ai[i] = inputs[i]


# hidden activations
  for j in range(self.hidden):
    sum = 0.0
    for i in range(self.input):
      sum += self.ai[i] * self.wi[i][j]
    self.ah[j] = sigmoid(sum)
  # output activations
  for p in range(self.output):
    sum = 0.0
    for j in range(self.hidden):
      sum += self.ah[j] * self.wo[j][p]
    self.ao[p] = sigmoid(sum)
  return self.ao[:]
```

The input activations will form our input features. However, for each of our layers, the activations should be the sum of the previous layers activations multiplied by their weight and then passed through a sigmoid function.

During the first pass, the predictions will be bad. That is why we will use the concept of gradient descent. In the case of a linear model, we should use a bit of calculus for the neural network. That is why we wrote the function of the derivative of our sigmoid function at the beginning.

The backpropagation algorithm will begin by computation of the error of the predicted output against true input. We can then take the derivative of our sigmoid on the output activations so as to get the direction of the gradient and then multiply the value by the error. We should then take the derivative of our input function on our output activations, so as to obtain the gradient direction and then multiply the value by the error we got. This will give us the magnitude of the error and the direction to which we should change the hidden weights to so as to correct it. We should then proceed to the hidden layer so as to calculate the error of hidden layer weights, and this will be determined by the magnitude and the error which we got in our previous calculation.

We can then use that error and the derivative of our sigmoid on our hidden layer activations to determine the amount and direction that our weights should change for the input layer.

Now that we have the values for the amount we need to change and the rates and the direction, we should continue to do that. The weights which connect each layer should then be updated. This should be done by multiplying the current weights with a constant of the learning rate and the direction and magnitude of the corresponding weight of the layers. We should use a constant for the learning rate just like in a linear model, so that only small changes can be made at each step, and we will have a great chance of getting the true values for our weights which can minimize the cost function. This is shown in the code given below:

def backPropagate(self, targets, N):
```
"""
```

:param targets: y values

```
    :param N: learning rate
    :return: the updated weights and the current error
    """
    if len(targets) != self.output:
        raise ValueError('You have wrong number of targets!')
    # calculating the error terms for the output
    # the delta will tell you the direction to change your
weights
    output_deltas = [0.0] * self.output
    for k in range(self.output):
        error = -(targets[k] - self.ao[k])
        output_deltas[k] = dsigmoid(self.ao[k]) * error
    # calculating the error terms for hidden
    # delta will tell you the direction to change your
weights
    hidden_deltas = [0.0] * self.hidden
    for j in range(self.hidden):
        error = 0.0
        for p in range(self.output):
            error += output_deltas[p] * self.wo[j][p]
        hidden_deltas[j] = dsigmoid(self.ah[j]) * error
    # updating the weights which connect the hidden to
the output
    for j in range(self.hidden):
        for p in range(self.output):
            change = output_deltas[p] * self.ah[j]
            self.wo[j][p] -= N * change + self.co[j][p]
            self.co[j][p] = change
    # updating the weights which connect the input to
the hidden
    for i in range(self.input):
        for j in range(self.hidden):
            change = hidden_deltas[j] * self.ai[i]
            self.wi[i][j] -= N * change + self.ci[i][j]
            self.ci[i][j] = change
    # calculating the error
    error = 0.0
    for k in range(len(targets)):
        error += 0.5 * (targets[k] - self.ao[k]) ** 2
```

return error

At this point, we can tie them together so as to create some training and prediction functions. The steps for training a network are very straightforward and intuitive. We can first call the function *"feedForwardFunc"* which will give us the outputs with randomized weights which we had initialized. We can then call the backpropagation algorithm for tuning and updating the weights for the purpose of making better predictions. The *"feedForwardFunction"* will then be called again but this time, it will make use of the updated weights, meaning that we will have better predictions. This cycle should be repeated for a number of times while reducing the error until we get a value for the error which tends to zero (o). This is shown in the example given below:

```
def train(self, patterns, iterations = 3000, N =
0.0002):
    # N: the learning rate
    for i in range(iterations):
        error = 0.0
        for p in patterns:
            inputs = p[0]
            targets = p[1]
            self.feedForward(inputs)
            error = self.backPropagate(targets, N)
        if i % 500 == 0:
            print('error %-.5f' % error)
```

Finally, we can work on the predict function. We call the *"feedForwardFunc"* which will give us the activation of our output layer. Do not forget that the activation of each of the layers is formed by combining the output of the previous layers, multiplied by their corresponding weights and then passed through a sigmoid function. This is shown in the code given below:

```
def predict(self, X):
    """
```

Return a list of predictions after the training algorithm
"""
```
    predictions = []
    for p in X:
      predictions.append(self.feedForward(p))
    return predictions
```

Once you run the code, you should get an accuracy of about 97%, which is a good percentage. You should now have the following as the complete code:

```
import math
import random
import numpy as np
np.seterr(all = 'ignore')

#the sigmoid transfer function
# when you are using the logit (sigmoid) transfer
function for our output layer ensure the y values have
been scaled from 0 to 1

# if you use the tanh for the output then you should
scale between -1 and 1

# we will use the sigmoid for output layer and tanh
for hidden layer
def sigmoid(x):
  return 1 / (1 + np.exp(-x))

# derivative of the sigmoid
def dsigmoid(y):
  return y * (1.0 - y)

# using tanh over the logistic sigmoid is good
def tanh(x):
  return math.tanh(x)

# derivative for the tanh sigmoid
def dtanh(y):
```

```python
        return 1 - y*y

class MLP_NeuralNetwork(object):
    """
    Has three layers: input, hidden and the output.
The input sizes and output must match the data

    the size of the hidden is user defined during
initialization of the network.
    The algorithm has to be generalized so as to be
usable on any dataset.

    As long as your data is in the format: [[[x1, x2, x3,
..., xn], [y1, y2, ..., yn]],

                        [[[x1, x2, x3, ..., xn], [y1, y2, ...,
yn]],

                        ...
                        [[[x1, x2, x3, ..., xn], [y1, y2, ...,
yn]]]
    The example provided below shows this with the
digit recognition dataset which has been provided

    Fully pypy compatible.
    """
    def __init__(self, input, hidden, output, iterations,
learning_rate, momentum, rate_decay):
        """
        :param input: number of the input neurons
        :param hidden: number of the hidden neurons
        :param output: number of the output neurons
        """
        # initialize the parameters
        self.iterations = iterations
        self.learning_rate = learning_rate
        self.momentum = momentum
        self.rate_decay = rate_decay

        # initialize the arrays
```

```python
        self.input = input + 1 # add 1 for the bias node
        self.hidden = hidden
        self.output = output

        # set up the array of 1s for the activations
        self.ai = [1.0] * self.input
        self.ah = [1.0] * self.hidden
        self.ao = [1.0] * self.output

        # create a randomized weights
        # use the scheme from 'efficient backprop for
initializing weights
        input_range = 1.0 / self.input ** (1/2)
        output_range = 1.0 / self.hidden ** (1/2)
        self.wi = np.random.normal(loc = 0, scale =
input_range, size = (self.input, self.hidden))

        self.wo = np.random.normal(loc = 0, scale =
output_range, size = (self.hidden, self.output))


        # create the arrays of 0 for the changes
        # this is essentially an array having temporary
values which gets updated during each iteration

        # based on the amount the weights want to
change in the next iteration

        self.ci = np.zeros((self.input, self.hidden))
        self.co = np.zeros((self.hidden, self.output))

    def feedForward(self, inputs):
        """
        The feedforward algorithm will loop over all the
nodes in hidden layer and add together all outputs
from input layer * their weights

        the output for each node will be the sigmoid
function of the sum of the inputs
```

and this is passed on to our next layer.

```python
        :param inputs: input data
        :return: the updated activation output vector
        """
        if len(inputs) != self.input-1:
            raise ValueError('You have wrong number of
inputs!')
        # the input activations
        for i in range(self.input -1): # -1 is for avoiding the
bias
            self.ai[i] = inputs[i]

        # the hidden activations
        for j in range(self.hidden):
            sum = 0.0
            for i in range(self.input):
                sum += self.ai[i] * self.wi[i][j]
            self.ah[j] = tanh(sum)

        # output activations
        for k in range(self.output):
            sum = 0.0
            for j in range(self.hidden):
                sum += self.ah[j] * self.wo[j][k]
            self.ao[k] = sigmoid(sum)

        return self.ao[:]

    def backPropagate(self, targets):
        if len(targets) != self.output:
            raise ValueError('You have wrong number of
targets!')

        # calculate the error terms for the output
        # the delta will tell you the direction to change
your weights
        output_deltas = [0.0] * self.output
        for k in range(self.output):
```

```
        error = -(targets[k] - self.ao[k])
        output_deltas[k] = dsigmoid(self.ao[k]) * error

    # calculate the error terms for the hidden
    # delta will tell you the direction to change your
weights
    hidden_deltas = [0.0] * self.hidden
    for j in range(self.hidden):
        error = 0.0
        for k in range(self.output):
            error += output_deltas[k] * self.wo[j][k]
        hidden_deltas[j] = dtanh(self.ah[j]) * error

    # updating the weights which connect the hidden
to the output
    for j in range(self.hidden):
        for p in range(self.output):
            change = output_deltas[p] * self.ah[j]
            self.wo[j][p] -= self.learning_rate * change +
self.co[j][p] * self.momentum

            self.co[j][p] = change

    # update the weights which connect the input to
the hidden
    for i in range(self.input):
        for j in range(self.hidden):
            change = hidden_deltas[j] * self.ai[i]
            self.wi[i][j] -= self.learning_rate * change +
self.ci[i][j] * self.momentum

            self.ci[i][j] = change

    # calculate the error
    error = 0.0
    for k in range(len(targets)):
        error += 0.5 * (targets[p] - self.ao[p]) ** 2
    return error
```

```python
def test(self, patterns):
    """

    Currently it will print out targets next to our
predictions.
    This is not useful for the actual ML, but just for a
visual inspection.
    """
    for p in patterns:
        print(p[1], '->', self.feedForward(p[0]))

def train(self, patterns):
    # N: learning rate
    for i in range(self.iterations):
        error = 0.0
        random.shuffle(patterns)
        for p in patterns:
            inputs = p[0]
            targets = p[1]
            self.feedForward(inputs)
            error += self.backPropagate(targets)
        with open('error.txt', 'a') as errorfile:
            errorfile.write(str(error) + '\n')
            errorfile.close()
        if i % 10 == 0:
            print('error %-.5f' % error)
        # learning rate decay
        self.learning_rate = self.learning_rate *
(self.learning_rate / (self.learning_rate +
(self.learning_rate * self.rate_decay)))


def predict(self, X):
    """

    Return the list of predictions after the training
algorithm
    """
    predictions = []
    for p in X:
        predictions.append(self.feedForwardFunc(p))
```

```python
    return predictions

def demo():
    """
    run N demo on digit recognition dataset
    """
    def load_data():
        data = np.loadtxt('Data/sklearn_digits.csv',
delimiter = ',')

        # the first ten values are the one hot encoded y
values
        y = data[:,0:10]
        #y[y == 0] = -1 # if using a tanh transfer function
just make the 0 to -1
        #y[y == 1] = .90 # try the values which won't
saturate tanh

        data = data[:,10:] # x data
        #data = data - data.mean(axis = 1)
        data -= data.min() # scale data so the values are
between 0 and 1
        data /= data.max() # scale

        out = []
        print data.shape

        # populate your tuple list with data
        for i in range(data.shape[0]):
            fart = list((data[i,:].tolist(), y[i].tolist())) # do
not mind the variable name

            out.append(fart)

        return out

    X = load_data()

    print X[9] # ensure that data looks right
```

```
NN = MLP_NeuralNetwork(64, 100, 10, iterations =
50, learning_rate = 0.5, momentum = 0.5, rate_decay
= 0.01)

NN.train(X)

NN.test(X)

if __name__ == '__main__':
    demo()
```

Regularization

Overfitting has become a major problem for Predictive Analytics and especially in neural networks. Regularization is one of the effective ways to prevent overfitting.

This method works by modifying the objective function which is minimized by adding some additional terms which penalize weights which are too large. In other words, the objective function is modified so as to become *"Error+$\lambda f(\theta)$,"* whereby the $f(\theta)$ will grow larger and larger as the components of the θ grow large. The λ will represent the strength of the regularization process, and it is a hyper parameter for our learning algorithm.

The value chosen for the λ will determine the amount that is needed for the purpose of reducing the overfitting. If we choose 0 as the value for the parameter, then this will be an indication that no step has been taken against overfitting. If we choose a large value for this parameter, then the focus will be on how to keep the θ as small as possible rather than focusing looking for the parameter values which will help training set experience a better performance. This shows how important choosing the λ parameter is and that we may be needed to perform a trial and error.

The L2 Regularization is the most common form of regulation used in neural networks. We can implement this by augmentation of the error function with a squared magnitude of all weights in your neural network. This means that for every weight "w" contained in the neural network, $1/2\ \lambda w^2$ should be added to the error function. The L2 regularization is good for the penalizing of the peaky weight vectors and then preferring the diffuse weight vectors. This is good for encouraging the network to make use of all of its inputs a little instead of making only a part of the inputs a lot. Note that during the process of a gradient descent update, the use of the L2 regularization will mean that each of the weights will be linearly decayed to zero. This explains the reason as to why L2 regularization is also referred to as weight decay.

The effects of L2 regularization can easily be visualized by use of ConvnetJs. Here, a neural network with two inputs is used with a size two soft-max output, and a hidden layer having 20 neurons. A mini-batch gradient descent is then used for the purpose of training the network (batch size of 20) together with 0.01, 0.1, and 1 for the regularization strengths.

L1 regularization is also another form of regularization which is commonly used. In this case, the term $\lambda|w|$ is added for every weight in our neural network. This phenomena has an effect that will cause the weight vectors to be sparse during the optimization process. This means that neurons using L1 regularization will only use a small part of their inputs, which make them become more resistant to the noise in the input.

To compare this, the weight vectors from L2 regularization are always diffuse, and small numbers. L1 regularization becomes important when you need to understand the exact features which contributed to a decision. If the feature at that level of analysis is not of importance, make use of the L2 regularization, since you will experience a better performance.

The max norm constraints usually have the same behavior of trying to restrict from θ of becoming too large, but this is done in a direct manner. These usually create an absolute upper bound on the size of the weight vector which is incoming for each neuron, and then use the projected gradient descent so as to enforce the constraint. The important property is that the parameter vector can't grow out of control since the updates to our weights are usually bounded, even when we have learning rates that are too high.

Dropout is another technique which can be used for the purpose of controlling overfitting. During training, this implemented by keeping a neuron active only with a probability "p", or otherwise, it is set to 0. This will force your network to be accurate even when it lacks some information. The network will also be prevented from becoming too dependent on anyone of the neurons or any of your small combinations. When expressed in a more mathematical way, it will prevent overfitting by providing a way to approximately combine the various neural network architectures more efficiently in an exponential manner.

Chapter 4- Improving a Neural Network in Python

Momentum

In neural networks, momentum is of importance, as it helps us in improving the performance of the stochastic gradient descent. The stochastic gradient descent will apply the following learning rule to each of the minibatches of data:

params := params - learning_rate * gradient

"params" represents the vector of parameters which define the model, the *"learning_rate"* is a scalar which will regulate the rate at which the parameters are updated, *"gradient"* is the gradient of objective function in respect to the parameters.

Momentum makes learning very effective. In this case, the parameters are moved with a certain velocity during every time step. The velocity will decay overtime exponentially with time, and the gradient can be added to it. Remember that velocity is a vector, meaning that the gradient is in a position to change both the magnitude and direction. The following is the learning rule for the momentum:

velocity := momentum_constant * velocity - learning_rate * gradient

params := params + velocity

The "momentum_constant" is a scalar which controls the rate at which the velocity will decay. Its value should be at least a 0. If it is set to exactly 0, then the momentum learning rule will reduce to the standard gradient descent learning rule. Also, note that the value for this constant should be set to a value which is less than 1.

Most people neglect the use of momentum which should not be the case. A stochastic gradient descent combined with momentum is the most descent way on how a neural network can be trained effectively. If you are using the stochastic gradient descent for the purpose of training a neural network, it is good for you to ensure that you are aware of how to use a momentum and then use it.

Momentum can easily be used in Pylearn2. In case you are using the SGD class for the purpose of using the stochastic gradient descent so as to train your neural network, you will only have to specify the argument for the learning rule in the SGD class. For you to use the momentum, set the argument to be the momentum object. The init momentum should be set to 0.5, as this is a best value for it.

With that, we will be sure that the learning algorithm will make use of the momentum learning rule, but the momentum_constant will remain constant for each of the learning steps. You should aim for increasing this value over time. This can be done by installing the MomentumAdjuster object into your extensions argument of Train object.

Chapter 5- Neupy

Consider the example given below:

```
from sklearn import cross_validation, metrics
from neupy import algorithms, layers, environment
from skdata.larochelle_etal_2007 import dataset

environment.reproducible()

rectangle_dataset = dataset.Rectangles()
rectangle_dataset.fetch(download_if_missing=True)

data, target = rectangle_dataset.classification_task()
x_train, x_test, y_train, y_test =
cross_validation.train_test_split(
    data, target, train_size=0.5
)

network = algorithms.MinibatchGradientDescent(
    [
        layers.Sigmoid(784),
        layers.Sigmoid(20),
        layers.RoundedOutput(1),
    ],
    error='binary_crossentropy',
    verbose=True,
    show_epoch=1,
    batch_size=1,
)
network.train(x_train, y_train, x_test, y_test,
epochs=10)

y_predicted = network.predict(x_test)
print(metrics.classification_report(y_test,
y_predicted))

roc_score = metrics.roc_auc_score(y_test,
y_predicted)
```

```
print("ROC score: {}".format(roc_score))

accuracy = metrics.accuracy_score(y_test,
y_predicted)

print("Accuracy: {:.2f}%".format(accuracy * 100))
```

The above example shows how Neupy can be used for implementation of a neural network.

Chapter 6- Models in Neural Networks

Multi-Layer Perceptron

MLP is a supervised learning algorithm which usually learns the function $f(\cdot) : R^m \rightarrow R^o$ after training it on a dataset, whereby "m" represents the number of the dimensions for the input and o represents the number of the dimensions for our output. Once you are given a set of features and a target, the MLP will learn the non-linear function approximator either for regression or classification. This is very different from logistic regression, and between the input and the output layer, we can have either one or even more non-linear layers, usually referred to as the hidden layers. Consider the example given below, which shows a MLP with one hidden layer and a scalar output.

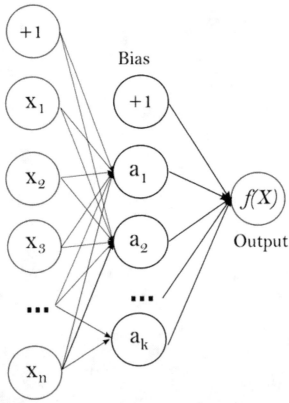

The leftmost layer is referred to as the *"input layer,"* and it is made up of a set of neurons which represent the input features. Each neuron in our hidden layer will transform the value obtained from the previous layer with a linear summation for the weight, which is then followed by a non-linear activation function just as the hyperbolic tan function. The output layer will receive the values from our last hidden layer, and then transform them to get the output values.

The following are some of the advantages of using a multi-layer perceptron:

1. Capability to learn the non-linear models.

2. Capability to learn the models in real-time by use of partial_fit.

However, despite these advantages, the MLP is very sensitive to feature scaling. It also requires us to tune a number of hyperparameters such as the number of the hidden neurons, iterations, and layers. MLPs having hidden layers usually contain a non-convex loss function in which there is more than one local minimum. This means that with different weight initializations, we may end up having different validation accuracy.

Classification

The class MLPClassifier is used for implementing a multi-layer perceptron algorithm which will be trained by use of the Backpropagation algorithm. Consider the example given below, which shows how a MLP can be trained:

```
>>> from sklearn.neural_network import MLPClassifier
>>> X = [[0., 0.], [1., 1.]]
>>> y = [0, 1]
```

```
>>> clf = MLPClassifier(algorithm='l-bfgs', alpha=1e-
5, hidden_layer_sizes=(5, 2), random_state=1)

>>> clf.fit(X, y)
MLPClassifier(activation='relu', algorithm='l-bfgs',
alpha=1e-05,
    batch_size='auto', beta_1=0.9, beta_2=0.999,
early_stopping=False,

    epsilon=1e-08, hidden_layer_sizes=(5, 2),
learning_rate='constant',

    learning_rate_init=0.001, max_iter=200,
momentum=0.9,
    nesterovs_momentum=True, power_t=0.5,
random_state=1, shuffle=True,

    tol=0.0001, validation_fraction=0.1,
verbose=False,
    warm_start=False)
```

Conclusion

We have come to the end of this guide. You should now be in a position to create your own neural network in Python. Note that neural networks work as a computing function in the same way as the neurons found in the human brain, hence the name. The network is made up of a number of layers, including the input layer, hidden layers, and the output layers. Our aim is to feed input at the input layer, and then wait for the output at the output layer, and determine the amount of error in the network. This should result in adjusting of the weights. Here, the backpropagation algorithm is used.